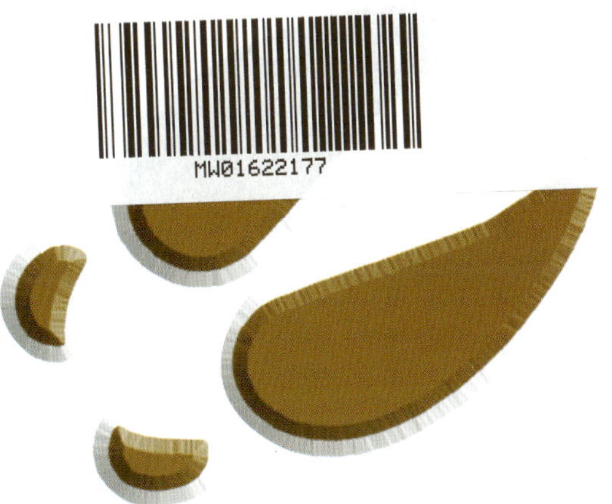

The Legend of Johnny Big Buck

SWIFT HILL

Jason R. Mumford

Please address inquiries about this book to the following:

PO Box 183 Girard, PA 16417 phone: 814/774-2171 fax: 814/774-0211
email: info@legendofjohnny.com www.legendofjohnny.com

First Printing 2005
Second Printing 2008

Also available from Sunnyside Publishing:
The Legend Whitetail Coloring Book
illustrated by Jason R. Mumford

See it online at www.legendofjohnny.com or buy it at your favorite outdoor retail store.

A NOTE TO OUR READERS:

After the release of our first edition, it came to our attention that the first portion of the book in which the characters go "spotting" or "shining" is a source of contention in the deer hunting community. We considered removing this portion prior to the second printing for that reason. We did not because the activity is an integral part of the deer hunting experience, for youngsters in particular, in New York and Pennsylvania. We understand why it is frowned upon by many hunters, and why it is illegal in many states. Spotting is indeed illegal in Pennsylvania during the rifle season. We in no way condone poaching deer or any other game animal. It is a disgraceful practice, and poachers should be prosecuted to the fullest extent of the law. Be assured in *The Legend* sequels, you will not see or read about spotting deer with an artificial light. Deer hunting is a great American heritage, and we are privileged to participate in it. It is our hope that this book helps to promote and encourage up-and-coming young hunters to enjoy, appreciate, and prolong deer hunting for many generations all across this great nation. Thanks for your support!

Sincerely,
Jason R. Mumford & Sunnyside Publishing Co.

Publisher's Catalog-In-Publication Data
Mumford, Jason R.
The Legend of Johnny Big Buck, Swift Hill
written and illustrated by Jason R. Mumford, Girard, PA
Sunnyside Publishing Co., © 2005, 2008

Printed in China

Summary: Five deer hunters spot and bow hunt a mature whitetail buck.

ISBN: 0-9769810-0-9
1. Whitetail buck--Juvenile fiction.

FOR TEAM HOUGHTON II

Caden, Jackson, Hunter, Brooke, Addison and Avery (so far…)

ACKNOWLEDGEMENTS:

Thank you Team Houghton - Cart, Robbie, Shane, and Paulie -
my brothers, for all the memories, deer hunts, for always being there...
and Kyle, all of the above goes for you as well, my friend.
Thanks to Charlie Alsheimer for your guidance, and for sharing your photos, expertise and passion for the whitetail with all of us.
Thank you Eric for sharing your technical savvy and for your patience with me.
To Jamie for the buck identification.
Words are simply an inadequate way to thank my wife and best friend Michele.
I love you more every day.
Thanks Anita, Heather, Angie, and Christi for being gracious hunting widows come October.
Thank you Lord God for blessing me with life and for instilling
within me a passion for Your creation,
and for putting me in a place where I am free to enjoy it.

Deep in the heart of whitetail deer country there lived a whitetail buck unlike any other. This deer was big - *really* big. Local farmers had glimpsed the buck in their fields late in the day. Experienced deer hunters realized this huge deer had survived many hunting seasons. He would know how to hide when they entered the woods with their bows and guns. This autumn, the heavy-racked buck would be four-and-a-half years old . . . and king of the deer woods!

The farmers' fields sparkled in the summer sun with healthy stalks of corn, soybeans and alfalfa. Many other deer were also seen in the fields as the evening sky faded from blue to gold to red. Soon, the days were short and the nights were cool. October arrived quickly, and so did deer hunting season!

The night before archery season, anticipation ran high for bow hunters in search of whitetails. Five hunters and best friends decided to spot the fields and look for deer. Rob, Paul, Jay and Shane piled into Carter's truck and drove off to find deer with spotlight in hand. As the guys rolled down the camp drive, gravel crunched under the big tire treads and dust curled into the cab through the open windows.

Rob coughed and said, “Let’s go out to Swift Hill. I was talking to a farmer at Joe’s gun shop yesterday and he said there was a big buck out there the other night.”

Everyone agreed, and on the way to Swift Hill they spotted the fields and saw many deer. With a gentle rumble, the pickup came to a halt next to a soybean field. Out popped the powerful spotlight, Paul flicked the switch, and the light revealed a nice eight-point and a big ten-point buck.

"Look at the split brow tines on that ten-point," whispered Jay. "I hope I see him in the woods tomorrow." Jay and the guys had waited all year for the opening day of archery season and this was just like Christmas Eve!

Carter slowly drove his big four-wheel drive truck down the dusty old dirt road past the woods at Swift Hill and pulled up between two big fields.

"Spot the field on the left, Robbie," said Paul. Rob swept the spotlight across the field.

"There's another buck!" said Jay. "Check it out with the binoculars, Paulie. It looks like another eight-pointer."

Paul looked at the buck through the binoculars as it bounded away toward the woods, trailing two does. Then, Rob swung the spotlight across the truck and lit up the field on the right. The field went uphill to a ridge about a hundred yards away. Robbie stopped the light on a pair of eyes at the top of the ridge.

"Look at that!" Shane rasped in a loud whisper.

There stood the most incredible whitetail buck anyone had ever seen. The farmers were right! His antlers were thick and heavy with a wide spread, sporting a lot of points. The deer's long, straight tines formed a beautiful rack with a long drop tine off the main beam of his right antler. The monster buck was awesome.

And then, he was gone. The huge whitetail made one leap and disappeared over the other side of the ridge. It was as if he was a ghost.

The friends sat amazed in the truck after seeing this massive buck. Rob went back and forth across the field with the spotlight, but the monster buck was nowhere to be seen.

"Did I just imagine that deer, or what?" asked Carter.

"If you did, I imagined it too," said Shane, shaking his head in disbelief.

"It was . . . Johnny Big Buck!" Rob proclaimed with wonder as he imagined hunting the buck the following morning.

Back at camp, each hunter prepared his bow, arrows, and other gear for the morning hunt. The guys talked about what might be the best way to hunt Johnny Big Buck.

"I hope it snows soon," said Carter, "I'll find his tracks and track him down."

"I think we should set up our treestands around that field, and then we'll get him when he comes out to feed," Paul explained.

"What time is it?" asked Rob.

"10:30," replied Paul.

"It is?" said Cart as he yawned, "I need to go to bed."

"No, Carter," Jay said. "Let's watch hunting videos!"

"Yeah, Cart," added Shane, "I have Old Mossy Volume 2. You should see this guy shoot right over Old Mossy's back!"

Carter agreed, so the five friends stayed up late watching hunting videos.

BEE-BEE-BEEEEEP went the alarm clock at 5:00 AM on the opening morning of archery season. The buddies crawled out of bed, left camp, and headed out to Swift Hill. Carter parked the truck just south of the fields. Everybody jumped out, put on their camos and grabbed their flashlights and bows. The hunt was on!

While it was still dark, everyone split up and found a place to stand and hunt around the fields. It was a cool, crisp October morning. The sun rose slowly over the eastern ridge, and the woods came alive with chirping chickadees and squirrels gathering nuts for the winter.

Carter set up in some woods mixed with pine trees and oaks at the corner of the field. As he watched a busy squirrel rustling through the leaves, he heard "*crunch-crunch-crunch!*" Cart slowly turned his head toward the sound of the crunching leaves and saw a big eight-point walking right toward him! The buck saw his movement, stopped, and looked right at Carter. Just then, the wind shifted and the deer caught his scent. The eight-pointer snorted and ran away, tail flagging.

"Nice buck!" said Cart, "but I would have passed him up anyway."

Carter was hunting Johnny Big Buck.

BM
1955
1900
SHANE
1900
Bear Run

At noon, everyone met back at the truck. Paul saw a little four-point and Shane saw three does, but no one saw Johnny Big Buck.

After lunch, Jay and Shane got out the topo map and mapped out a route to still hunt in the afternoon. The others went back out to find new places to stand. Jay and Shane made a big loop deep into the woods.

As the sun sank toward the horizon, Jay and Shane walked quietly through some thick pines and came to a grassy area. Thirty yards in front of them, a shrubby little tree was whipping back and forth in the weeds. A slight breeze quietly moved the blades of grass, but the little tree was moving too quickly. Something did not seem right.

"What is that?" Jay asked quietly.
"I don't know," said Shane,
"maybe there's an animal
stuck in there."

The two hunters watched this little tree for about ten seconds when suddenly Shane noticed huge antlers flying up and down, slashing the little tree to shreds!

"Buck!" whispered Shane, with his eyes fixed on the tree-destruction. He had an arrow nocked and immediately drew his bow.

Jay looked again and saw three or four long tines come up out of the weeds. It was him! Johnny Big Buck was making a rub on this little tree! Jay nocked an arrow and drew his bow.

They slowly stepped toward the giant whitetail, ready to shoot. All at once, the little tree stood still and everything was strangely quiet. Like a rocket, Johnny Big Buck exploded from the weeds and jumped away!

Shane pulled the trigger on his release and let his broadhead-tipped arrow fly. He watched it sail right over the huge deer's shoulder. Jay fired his arrow and saw it zip right behind the monster buck's tail, burying the tip in a tree trunk. The hunters listened while Johnny Big Buck crashed through the brush as he bolted away.

A few seconds later, the woods were quiet. Johnny Big Buck was gone again.

Shane and Jay just stood there quietly. They both had missed the buck of a lifetime.

After the last few rays of daylight faded from the horizon, everyone made their way out of the woods and met back at Carter's truck. The friends listened in disbelief as Jay and Shane told their amazing hunting story: seeing Johnny Big Buck demolish the little tree, missing him, and then watching the huge antlers disappear into the tangled brush.

“That is unbelievable!” said Rob.

Jay threw his hands up and said, “You imagine getting a shot at a deer like that your whole life, and then I miss! I don't think I am going to sleep tonight. Every time I close my eyes, I see my arrow flying past his tail!”

“I can't believe I missed, either - right over his back!” said Shane.

“All right, here's what we'll do: let's go and scout and find out where he's been traveling,” Rob replied as he explained his plan. “Maybe we can find more rubs and scrapes and set up on him again.”

“I don't know, Robbie. This buck is smart,” said Paul. “Do you guys think we'll see him again?”

Shane replied, “Sooner or later, he’ll make a mistake. When he does, we’ll get him!”

The five hunters packed up their gear and drove back to camp. Jay and Shane hung their heads in the back of the truck, hoping to get another shot at the monster buck. Cart said, "Hey man, I've missed more than one nice buck. You'll get another chance."

Then Jay and Shane realized they were not unsuccessful. They were able to see and shoot at a beautiful whitetail buck up-close. Even if he did get away, this opening day would be one to remember. And Johnny Big Buck would live to see another day that hunting season.

. . . to be continued!

Rub

Scrape

The Legend

www.legendofjohnny.com